W9-CFV-419

I Can Smell

Julie Murray

Abdo
SENSES
Kids

abdopublishing.com

Published by Abdo Kids, a division of ABDO, PO Box 398166, Minneapolis, Minnesota 55439.
Copyright © 2016 by Abdo Consulting Group, Inc. International copyrights reserved in all countries.
No part of this book may be reproduced in any form without written permission from the publisher.

Printed in the United States of America, North Mankato, Minnesota.

052015

092015

 THIS BOOK CONTAINS
RECYCLED MATERIALS

Photo Credits: iStock, Shutterstock

Production Contributors: Teddy Borth, Jennie Forsberg, Grace Hansen

Design Contributors: Candice Keimig, Dorothy Toth

Library of Congress Control Number: 2014958412

Cataloging-in-Publication Data

Murray, Julie.
 I can smell / Julie Murray.
   p. cm. -- (Senses)
ISBN 978-1-62970-927-7
Includes index.
1. Smell--Juvenile literature.   I. Title.
612.8′6--dc23

                                    2014958412

Table of Contents

I Can Smell

There are five senses.

Smell is one of the senses.

5

We smell with our noses.

We smell things all around us!

We smell flowers.

Cole smells the roses.

We smell food.

Lily smells the pizza.

We smell good things.

Sara smells cookies **baking**.

We smell stinky things.

Luke smells his shoes.

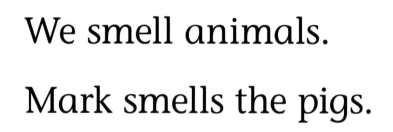

We smell animals.

Mark smells the pigs.

We smell fresh air.

Kate takes a deep **breath**.

What did you smell today?

The Five Senses

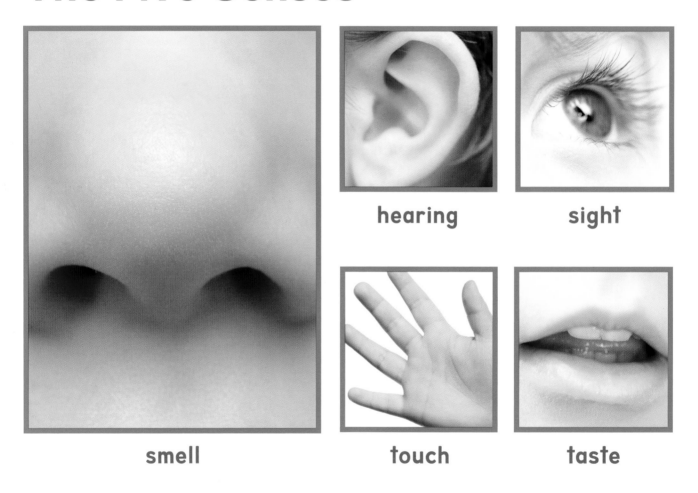

smell

hearing

sight

touch

taste

Glossary

bake
to cook food in an oven using heat.

breath
the air that you take into your lungs and let out when you breathe.

Index

abdokids.com

Use this code to log on to abdokids.com and access crafts, games, videos, and more!

Abdo Kids Code:
SIK9277